Origami Book for Beginners

A Guide to Craft 25 Easy Paper Folding Designs with Step by Step Instructions | Paper Crafts for Kids and Adults

By

Angelica Lipsey

Copyright © 2021 – Angelica Lipsey

All rights reserved

No part of this publication may be reproduced, distributed, or transmitted in any form or by any means, including photocopying, recording, or other electronic or mechanical methods, without the prior written permission of the publisher, except in the case of brief quotations embodied in reviews and certain other non-commercial uses permitted by copyright law.

Disclaimer

This publication is designed to provide competent and reliable information regarding the subject matter covered. However, the views expressed in this publication are those of the author alone, and should not be taken as expert instruction or professional advice. The reader is responsible for his or her own actions.

The author hereby disclaims any responsibility or liability whatsoever that is incurred from the use or application of the contents of this publication by the purchaser or reader. The purchaser or reader is hereby responsible for his or her own actions.

Table of Contents

Introduction 7

Chapter 1 10

The Basics of Origami Art 10

    What is Origami? 11

    History of Origami 14

    Benefits of Origami 20

    Application Areas of Origami 25

Chapter 2 28

Common Terms Used in Origami Art 28

Chapter 3 43

Tips and Tricks Used in Origami 43

Chapter 4 59

Getting Started with Origami 59

    Tools and Materials Used in Origami 59

        Origami Paper 59
        Paper Folding Tool 65

    Scoring Tool 66
    Glue 67
    Ruler 67
    Scissors 67
    Paper Clips 68
  Basic Origami Folding Symbols 69

  Common Origami Bases 70

  Basic Origami Folds 75

Chapter 5 81

Origami Project Ideas 81

  DIY Crane Garland 82

  Heart Escort Card 84

  Heart Page Marker 86

  Butterfly 89

  Heart Origami 92

  Halloween Design 95

  Paper Star 99

  Origami Boat 102

  Origami Lampstand 104

Lotus Flower 106

DIY Ice Cream Origami 109

Pencil Holder 112

Paper Flower 114

Paper Clutch 117

Flower Vase 120

Christmas Tree Décor 123

Butterflies 127

Envelope 131

Candy Purse 133

Kusudama Flower 135

Origami Roses 138

Origami Card Holder 140

Bear Head 144

Wet Folding Project 147

Chapter 6 153

Frequently Asked Questions in Origami 153

Conclusion 160

Introduction

Origami is one fascinating art that has so many benefits to just about anyone. Unlike many crafts, it is stress-free, simple and very beneficial to all ages. Irrespective of your profession, age, level of education, creative and locomotive abilities, as well as your experience in craft making, you can become a master in origami.

This is one of the simplest crafts you will ever try. In no time and with little stress, you can produce an art piece of all time. Asides from making art pieces, origami is also used to teach some essential life skills to little children, teenagers and adults.

With consistency and practice, a little child could learn origami perfectly and all the little skills it proposes to teach. This is why many schools have adopted it into their curriculum, even parents now teach it to their children at home.

If you have a little child around you, this could be one of the best gifts you can give to them, as these skills stay with them forever and help them stand out from their peers. Amongst other things, it sharpens their intellectuality.

Who won't want to raise a smart, intelligent young child? Such a child will definitely become a worldwide asset and the delight of every nation. It might not appear like something huge, but mental development is highly underrated in many places. Unfortunately, many persons are ignorant of its importance in a child's life and the adverse benefit to the society at large. This is why I'm extremely glad that you have taken the wise step to get this book for yourself and I enjoin you to read all the explanations and instructions carefully laid out in this book. Also, do well to study all the illustrations you find here; they will help you cement all the theoretical knowledge detailed herein in the chapters.

Origami is practiced in almost all countries of the world, starting from middle Asia to Europe and then all other continents. Today, it is one of the most popular art around the world. Also it has been acknowledged as a commonly practiced art in many foreign countries. No need to give you statistics; if you look around you, you will see paper art products. This was not so many years ago, paper art has greatly advanced and there are more interesting arts, unlike the basic ones that were common in those days.

As an artist, you can invent your own paper art design and make good money from it. You could also teach it to others for money or get yourself hired as a school teacher to teach it to kids. You could also get hired to decorate a wedding using your origami skills.

With this book, you can have a great and clean start in origami art and make that fancy design you've always admired. You can turn your plain walls into a beautiful and interesting sight and cause visitors to wow as they admire your handiwork. Get ready to be drowned in a world of creativity. Join me as I explicitly expose you to the intricacies of origami in the pages of this book.

Chapter 1

The Basics of Origami Art

Origami is the most practiced paper folding art in the records of history. It is a highly creative art that just anyone can do, whether you are innately creative or not. Commonly taught in schools today, it is far beyond a classroom curriculum. Most people practice origami for fun, but as a master, you could earn from it. However, money shouldn't be your goal for learning this craft; you could easily lose motivation if you place your inspiration on money. Making money from origami is a possibility that you can gain access to as a master, and to be a master, you have to be deeply passionate about this craft. It all starts with passion. Join me as we begin to explore the basics of this art. We will be looking at its definition and history to provide you with a balanced and beyond fundamental knowledge of what origami is about. We would also be looking at the benefits and applications to set your heart aflame with passion for the journey of knowledge still ahead.

What is Origami?

Origami is the long-aged art of paper folding into decorative and representative forms. Some of these representative forms are animals, flowers, objects, etc. It is a popular practice that has left an expensive paper trail across the globe. This fine art started in Asian countries many years ago and has transcended into becoming a culture in many localities. Today it is a renowned Japanese culture.

The name origami is derived from Japanese words; ori, which means folding and kami, which means paper. It was initially known as orikata, which meant folded shapes. The name was changed to origami in 1880. It involves the use of paper to make beautiful artworks through folding. Local origami simply involves folding a sheet of colored square paper into a sculpture. There is no cutting, gluing, marking, or taping. The square paper is folded several times and arranged until it fits into the desired shape.

Paper folding is a once highly underestimated art that is gaining so much relevance today. The paper was folded with different techniques into various shapes. The goal is to transform the flat sheet of craft paper into a finished artistic sculpture. Most of these sculptures were made with the use of glue, cuts or markings on the picture.

Origami ranges from super complex with realistic models to simple models that are very easy to make and recognizable. Depending on the model, it can be easy or difficult. This craft is likewise practiced as a hobby by many persons, including the young and old, especially in places like Europe. It could also be mind-bending or relaxing, depending on the type of folding you engage in and your reasons for folding.

Today many people of different age brackets are attracted to this form of art because paper is now one of the cheapest craft supply. Origami was first viewed as craft for the elites because paper was far from being affordable many years ago. It wasn't until the beginning of the twentieth century that this changed and paper became relatively affordable by the average man.

Early Japanese monks used origami models for religious purposes, and the Chinese used them for traditional and ceremonial purposes. There were different forms of origami practiced by the Japanese in those days; folding butterflies-shaped papers was a Japanese traditional wedding décor. There were also folds of paper gift wrappers in Tsutsnami used in many traditional ceremonies as a symbol of modesty and sincerity. Folded sheets of paper were common ceremonial models, especially at weddings.

Few years down the line, paper became a cheap commodity and people started making origami models as gifts to their loved ones. People also started to create folded paper cards and envelopes for correspondence. Paper art gradually transcended into an educational activity for school children to boost their creativity and mathematical abilities.

Though, origami is directly traced to Japan, art lovers from several countries helped shape origami until it grew into a popular practice that it is today. It is more beautiful when the folds are of different colors.

Origami is a very flexible art, and it is highly innovative and creative. You could do anything with your inspiration. Although it still has some guidelines and principles that cannot be broken despite its flexibility. Origami must forever reside in the borders of folds.

There are simple principles being practiced in origami. These principles are also practiced in stents, packaging, and other engineering applications. They will be discussed explicitly in the coming chapters.

Let's move on to review the history of Origami.

History of Origami

Paper invention was successful in China around 105 AD. After many years of paper invention, folded paper art known as zhezhi emerged. Around 900 AD, paper yuanboo became a staple in traditional Chinese funerals.

This art is created by meticulously making folds of ingot currency with gold or yellow colored paper. These ornaments are crafted with the aim to be thrown into the fire after the ceremony. It was an ephemeral art temporarily for decorating the ceremony.

They eventually started doing long term arts to decorate their rooms. This art was advanced into making inanimate objects like boats and boxes. The artists began exploring different forms of paper folding art and trying out other forms of art. They created many captivating art and held several exhibits where they displayed their creative art and started paper folding as a common practice.

It wasn't long when it became a culturally recognized art.

Paper was invented in Japan in late 6th century. Paper folding started as a ceremonial ritual called Shinto ritual. This art is a native practice that was performed ceremonially as a ritual every year. The Shinto festival involved folding colorful papers into paper models of a simple butterfly design. This design or ritual was also done in traditional wedding ceremonies. Asides wedding ceremonies, folding was very common in some ceremonial functions in Japanese culture during the Edo period. It was a ceremonial practice that everyone engaged in at the time. The simplicity of the craft enhanced its popularity. Many years later down to the 15th century, during the Japan's Edo period (1603-1868) origami grew more popular and became a leisure activity and expression of art. One of the best-known origami model is the Japanese paper crane.

It transcended from a cultural activity to an artwork. These artworks usually include nature-based motifs like flowers and birds. They are all still prevalent and popular in contemporary origami. Initially, they made simple art by strategically cutting paper sheets to various shapes and making inscriptions on them. Some form of origami arts involved drawing things on paper and cutting it to the shape of the drawing, to paste on the wall. Some of these inscriptions are instructive and admonishing. They are usually placed in the part of the house where everyone can see them. These subjects are popular in contemporary origami. The modern Japanese practice still involves those traditional origami folds. Although, it has transcended from plain cutting of papers to folding of sheets into various shapes. This style of paper art was adopted firsthand from Europe.

True origami, according to experts, is sculpted entirely through folds. Today, origami is being practiced as a serious art and sculptures are being sculptured entirely throughout Japan. Many years ago, a traditional Japanese story says that if a person folds 1000 papers of origami models, they will be granted a special wish. This story was the inspiration that led many persons to practice origami.

In Europe, origami became a popular practice in the 17th century. The practice has been on for several years before then, but it wasn't popular. Paper folding happened to evolve from napkin folding. The European maids used to fold the napkin on the dining table. Napkin fold was a status symbol of nobility. This napkin folding technique was well practiced until the 18th century, when it was replaced by porcelain. Porcelain was quite an expensive piece, so it took time before it totally displaced napkin folds. The practice of napkin folding started to disappear by the day until a few individuals decided to try out the art on paper. Paper proved to be far easier to fold than napkin and allows for deeper creativity. They started using the paper for art and started featuring different techniques, just like the Japanese.

The Europeans began folding the paper with different techniques into abstractly innovative and figurative forms. The practice of folding papers like napkins at dinner parties transcended into schools in Europe. This art was added to the school's curriculum by Friedrich Froebel and taught as a subject to kindergarten. Because of the simplicity of the art, it was easy to teach it to small children of age 5 and above. Origami for children includes hands-on activities of folding paper just like napkin. These activities involved just simple techniques. Hence, it was very easy for children to attain familiarity with the art all over the continent. Origami eventually became a homely art that many persons practiced in different parts of the continent.

This art began to flourish well in western Europe. It was carried on and spread throughout the globe by the children themselves in their homes. These different techniques of art became a common craft in early Europe. It still is today. When the Japanese opened their border in 1860, they adapted Froebel's kindergarten system. That was where they adapted the different cuts method and started to use bi-colored square papers.

Before this time, Japanese origami involved various simple shapes, with cuts and coloration or markings. These styles became extinct and a new form of origami was added to the Japanese tradition and culture.

The history of origami cannot be fully discussed without the mention of Akira Yoshizawa. He was the one who advanced origami till it became a worldwide craft. He transformed a local, religious craft into a highly respected and valued craft.

A Japanese man, Akira Yoshizawa, in the early 1900s, began creating and recording original origami works. Akira was often addressed as the grandmaster of origami. He learned origami as a little child far back early 20th century. With this knowledge and depth in origami, he taught some co-factory employees the geometric concepts needed to complete their respective jobs. In 1994, he released his first book on origami, known as Atarashi Origami Geijutsu (New Origami Art). The book carefully listed and described symbols or notations used in folding different forms of fold. This book helped spread his fame and turned him into an origami superstar and catalyst. He began to advance origami at a very young age by teaching it directly in conferences and seminars. He is the father of several innovations, such as wet-folding, which involves spraying water on paper to create a rounder appearance. His innovation birthed many more innovations and renaissance of the art form. In 1980, origami transcended beyond a simple art into a more complex and highly creative craft as some distinguished persons started to systematically study the mathematical relationship. This led to serious complexity of the origami models. The models were more complex and technical.

Akira spent the late years of his life as a cultural ambassador for Japan. He was also regarded as the person who brought stronger awareness of unique origami techniques to a large part of the world. Five years ago, a book named Akira Yoshizawa was published, featuring all of his works. He created over 50,000 different paper figures in his lifetime. Since he died in 2005, there is hardly anyone to beat that number of paper figures. He is indeed the father of origami.

Europe, China, and Japan are well-documented historians of distinct paper folding traditions.

The advancement of origami is directly traceable to Japan; they were the first persons to discover the usefulness of paper as a medium of arts. There have been a lot of variations to the art today, cutting gluing to increase the stability of the design and allowing for more flexibility and adaptability.

The debate on using adhesives has been settled and technology has allowed for great advancement and modernization. Also, the type of paper used in origami has been modernized. People do craft with scrap papers like old newspapers. These days, people work with wrapping paper, typing paper and other handmade paper. Hence, allowing more creativity and innovations. From now on, paper art is certain to advance more than it is now and become a great commercial craft tomorrow. Although some historians state that origami started in China, history stated that it flourished in Japan.

Benefits of Origami

Origami is a highly creative art with applications in the classroom for students and serves as a decorative piece in the house. Talking about its application in the classroom, researchers have found many ways that origami can make lessons enticing and enhance students' learning of the skills they need.

It is important for teaching geometry; some instructors use it to illustrate geometry in mathematics, using the curves and edges for explanations. According to NCES (National Center for Education), in 2003, American students had struggles with geometry. It was one academic weakness they all had in many locations. Origami aids in strengthening and granting an explicit understanding of geometric concepts, formulas, labels and making them come alive. It enhances the student's understanding of the concept, area, perimeters and circumference of shapes. Increase in thinking skills is also a benefit of Origami. It has been proven to improve spatial visualization skills using hands-on learning. Using origami helps the children comprehend, construct and characterize their own vernacular for the world around them. Explaining geometric terms using origami enhances their thinking ability.

Origami helps to illustrate fractions for better understanding: You could also explain fractions in a tactile way using origami. You can use paper to display different types of fractions by folding it one-half, or one-fourth.

It builds problem-solving skills: Making origami could prove to be quite challenging to the children. Challenging the children to make origami projects themselves can help improve their problem-solving skills and thinking abilities, just like quantitative reasoning. The child knows that it is remaining only one fold to make the perfect model, but where and how to make the fold is also something to think about.

It improves 3D perception and logical thinking: Origami helps your perception and improves your logical thinking. Making 3D projects could be really challenging, especially for small children. However, the more you expose them to it, the more result you get.

Creative ability: Origami helps increase your creative ability. Even though you weren't born creative, you can always learn. You don't have to make an elephant model already. You want to hone your creativity, start from the supposedly simple and basic origami projects for kids and adults; a number of them are listed in this book. The more you make the folds, the more your creativity is sharpened.

It is simply fun: another beautiful benefit of origami is fun! I love fun activities; I guess everyone does too. I sincerely haven't met anyone that is averse to fun, which reaffirms my statement that origami is for everyone—irrespective of your age. For children, there are several projects they can engage in to make their own items for play. This is why paper planes remain the number one child-friendly origami project. Every child will love to see something fly in the air while they chase it about. Talk more of when they are to make it themselves. It is thrilling and more fun for them.

It helps you relax and deal with stress: I recommend this for aged people or mature adults prone to stress. Origami is the most stress-free craft, as you can make the world's most beautiful origami pieces just by sitting on one seat. Even as an aged person, you could make simple projects that will help you deal with stress and help your body relax while exercising your mind.

Other educational benefits of origami are:

Eye-hand coordination: Origami, like every other basic craft, teaches eye-hand coordination and boosts kids' smartness.

Sequencing skills: Every project contains well-outlined steps that should be followed in a particular order. Any child that practices origami will be able to do sequencing well.

Maths reasoning: There are technical origami projects that require calculations, hence, while working on them, it sharpens a person's calculative abilities and improves maths reasoning.

Spatial skills: Again, origami teaches you the positioning of things as well as organization. It is a good means to teach children organization.

Patience and attention skills: Children are easily distracted and impatient when it comes to getting something done, especially when it isn't something they find fun. Origami is an interesting craft that will help capture your child's attention while teaching them patience, amongst other skills. It also sharpens mental concentration.

Enhances teamwork: Most children, after they learn, move on to teach their friends too with pride. Hence, it helps to build that teaching and team leadership skill in the children. They are not just waiting to be taught all the time, but moving on to teach others themselves.

Also, some origami projects could require teamwork, hence building team spirit.

Finally, research has it that students who use origami perform better in science-related courses.

Application Areas of Origami

As I have listed amongst the benefits, origami is very useful in teaching math and science subjects. The art of origami is widely spread and has happened to catch young people's and adults' attention. It helps an individual develop many skills just by the simple art of folding paper to make shapes of different forms using basic tools.

Origami is majorly applied for STEAM; Science, technology, engineering, art, and math.

In science, origami is majorly used in medicine.

In technology, origami is used in developing new technological systems.

In engineering, origami is used to plan constructions.

In art: origami is used for decoration.

In math: origami is used to illustrate geometry and calculations.

Other forms of applications are explained below:

Symmetry: Majority of origami patterns require symmetrical work. Origami is used to teach symmetry.

Measurement and Geometry: It is used to teach measurement and show geometrical shapes like triangle and square. It is also used to teach fractions & proportions.

Mathematics: School teachers use origami as an instructional tool in education that helps in explaining and solving fractions and geometric or mathematical problems.

Medicine: It is used to embody the cell membrane and protein used in modeling DNA samples.

Mechanical engineering: Origami is used to make pipes that are used in Japanese high-speed trains. This special inner pipe is used to absorb pressure, hence reducing the risk of road accidents.

Space technology: There are future plans to launch an aircraft into space using origami techniques. The instruments and plan have been drafted and tested several years ago. Origami is also used to solve huge problems in technology.

Architecture and civil engineering: Sometimes, origami designs and techniques are used by engineers to create designs. Architects also use it to create miniature models of stadiums and bridges.

Décor: Asides from the above applications, decoration is another most common use of origami. Many designs are used to make letters and gifts, 3D shapes, toys, exterior, and interior decoration.

Chapter 2

Common Terms Used in Origami Art

Like in every craft, there are basic terms that are commonly used in the craft's practice. Origami being an aged long craft, has a large number of terms that are commonly used. I have outlined and briefly explained some of these terms. A few of these terms are Chinese and Japanese words used to define certain techniques in Origami. Some of them will be explained in detail in the coming chapters.

You don't need to worry yourself about cramming all the 30 plus terms. It is only important that you are familiar with them, so you won't be at a loss when you see them while practicing. Hence, endeavor to pay attention to all of the terms listed herein and familiarize yourself with them.

Action model: An action model is a design that is responsive when completed. It is the opposite of a decorative piece; an action model is designed for action and is expected to be mobile. A common example is a paper plane or a bird with wings. This model is highly artistic and simply creative.

Kasane Origami: This is a Japanese term for layered origami where many sheets of paper are overlapped and arranged decoratively.

Surface: This is the top layer of the paper. Every plain sheet of paper has two surfaces.

Black coating: This is the gluing of two separate sheets to form a single solid sheet.

Knotologie: This is a technique applied in folding long strips of paper. This technique was developed by an Austrian folder named Heinz Strobl.

Base: This is the combination of folds that are used as a starting point for folding and creating artistic projects.

The fish base: This base is characterized by two long rabbit-earing in two separate corners along the diagonal of the paper. It has four flaps: two long and two short.

Swivel fold: This is a folding technique that involves moving paper in many different directions.

Tissue foil: A technique where tissue is glued to either side of a sheet of paper. This helps the foil to be malleable and have a more natural finish.

The kite base: This is a simple base with three creases made from folding along the diagonal of the square, unfolding the folds and then refolding two adjacent sides to line up with the diagonal. The result is a kite or ice cream cone shape.

A4: This is a rectangular paper that has its sides in the proportion of 1, root 2. This paper is very malleable and is commonly used only in basic projects. It is rarely used in any major or complex project because of its fragility.

Bird base: This base is formed by petal folding both sides of a preliminary base; it is the starting point of a crane. There are four triangular points; one is short at the center and the other three are longer.

Stretched bird base: This technique is used to give the bird base a displaced look. It is formed by pulling apart the wingtips of the bird base. This looks like the bird is about to take flight.

Kirigami: This is a Japanese word for cutting papers where shapes are produced by cutting a paper's pre-folded sheet.

Kirikomi origami: This term means that the cuts in a paper are used to extend the range of folding possibilities in a standard origami model.

The book base: This is the simplest traditional base, also referred to as a book fold. It is made by bringing one edge of a square or rectangle to the opposite edge, folding the sheet in half.

Book fold: A fold that involves folding one side of a square opposite to the other. This fold moves a flap from one side to another.

The cupboard base: This is one of the most basic traditional origami bases. This fold is made joining two opposite edges of a square to the centerline; two unique bases have been made from here: pinwheel base and pig base.

Tension: This is where a paper is held in a particular position by using certain natural strength or tension from within the paper.

Kite fold: Kite fold is a basic fold of a paper square in which creases are made after two adjacent edges of the paper are placed along a diagonal.

Blintz base: To fold all four corners of a square into the centre. This is a traditional origami base named after a thin pancake of Slavic origins. It is used as a type of fold in bringing all four corners to the center as a verb. Other bases were derived from it.

Square/ preliminary base: This is a starting point for the frog and bird basses.

Frog base: This simple origami base has four short and four long triangular flaps.

Waterbomb base: This traditional base has five sharp points. One short point at the middle and four long points at the sides, the shape is likened to a flattened pyramid.

Twist folding: This technique was developed by a Japanese folder named Shuzo Fujimoto; it allows paper to be pleated and collapsed in a twisted form.

Valley fold: This is a type of crease made by folding a paper towards you.

Landmark: This is a corner or an intersection of creases.

Box-pleating: A technique that pleats the paper and collapses it into straight points. This technique was developed by an American folder named Neal Elias.

Bronco sinkin: This term is not so popular, but it is a name given to an origami figure that is a master in his craft.

Canson: A brand of French paper ideal for wet-folding.

Treemaker: This term is used to name a computer program by Robert Lang and used to design origami bases. This is achieved by drawing a stick figure on the screen. A stick represents a flap on the base. Once you define the type of tree, the computer computes the full crease pattern for a base.

Wet folding: A popular technique used to give foreign shapes. It was invented by Akira Yoshizawa.

Chapeaugraphy: The folding of a felt ring into shapes representing hats.

Fold: This term means to bring two parts of a piece of paper into contact. It is also defined as the flattening of paper.

Pure or True origami: This form of origami is a style of origami where the paper isn't cut, glued or decorated. It is plain origami. It is still practiced in some native parts.

Pureland origami: This type of origami is limited to mountain and valley folds. This origami was invented by a British paper folder named John Smith.

Waterbomb: This is a term used to describe an inflated fold that looks like a square container and can be filled with water to be hauled at someone.

Washi: A popular handmade paper from Japan. This paper is made from the bark of trees. It is one of the most commonly used origami paper.

Circular origami: The use of circular paper in place of square paper for origami.

Location fold: This is a point or place in a sheet where a corner or edge should meet in order to complete that fold.

Pre-creasing: Pre-creasing is a technique of adding creases upon creases then unfolding all the creases. The unfolded creases are used in a sequence to complete the model.

Maneuver: When different folds are combined together to produce a particular result, such as a rabbit's ear or a very creative or folded design, it is called a maneuver.

Foil: This is a paper with metal foil on one surface and ordinary paper on the other. A number of paper folders recommend it for certain technical projects because of its sensitivity. A beginner cannot use this paper as it is easily condemnable.

RAT: This is an abbreviation that means 'right about there.' It is used to mark out a point where no location creases exist.

Raw edge: This is an edge of a single layer of a sheet of paper with one of the original edges outside the square.

Rabbit's ear: This is a technique that forms just a small triangular flap.

Closed sink: If a standard sink cannot be made on a paper by unfolding, it must be gently forced in, this technique is called a closed sink.

Folding geometry: The specific geometric properties, e.g., types of angles, on a paper fold's crease pattern.

Minimalist origami: This is a type of origami in which the design to be made is sketched rather than photographed. This type of origami is done to reduce the number of folds.

Duo: A colorful paper with two colors on either side.

Fold line: This line represents valley creases, a dash and two dots represent a mountain fold. It is used in origami diagrams.

Collapse: The series of pre-creases when they are in place. You can place the paper into a new arrangement of layers.

Folded edge: This is a sharp edge where two individual layers are joined.

Model: Some folders call this design. This term refers to a finished item of origami.

Windmill fold: A simple fold where the origami paper is configured to the shape of a pinwheel or windmill.

X-ray view: This gives a clear view of crease lines that are hidden and invincible. This technique is usually indicated in origami instructional diagram.

Elephant hide: This is not the skin of an elephant as it seems, but a type of paper made in Germany and used in special origami projects.

Crane: This is the most common fold in origami, it has an appearance of a flapping bird, and a technical process makes it by narrowing the head and tail. This is one project every beginner mustn't fail to attempt.

Fabrigami: This is the folding of origami models using hard fabric or fabric bonded to paper. Just like the name depicts, Fabric and Origami.

Crease: This is a sharp or blunt line formed on a paper by folding.

Minor miracle: This is a technique where there are two flaps on the two sides of the folded paper; one of the flaps is folded to the front and back left.

Fish base: This is a technical base used as a starting point for folding a fish and other related models.

Crease pattern: This pattern is achieved by unfolding all the folds in an origami model.

Flapping bird: This is the more complex design made from the bird base. It is a representation of a tiny bird whose wings can flap.

Cupboard fold: This is the folding of two opposite edges to form a crease at the center of the paper.

Blintz fold: In this fold, all four corners of a paper's square sheet are brought to the center point.

Petal fold: The petal fold is a basic technique where a layer of paper is lifted up and the sides are narrowed to form a point. It is used mostly in flower designs.

Kami paper: This is a high-quality origami paper. One of the best there is.

Flexagon: This is paper folded in regular angles so that the face is hidden inside and can only be revealed by turning the paper inside out.

Inverted: This is a point where a flap has been turned in such a way that the inside is out.

Iso-area folding: This is a type of fold, which when completed, displays an equal amount of the front and back color of the paper.

Multi-piece origami: This technique creates subjects of a model from one sheet of paper and more. For instance, the hand and feet might be designed using different papers.

Book folder: This tool is traditionally used for bookbinding. It is made from bone or plastic. Some are made from Teflon woods or other materials. It is used to create a consistent and noticeable sharp crease. It is also used to manipulate the paper in technical ways that cannot be done with the hands, like probing small spaces in the model. A common bone folder is about 6 inches long, 1-inch-wide, a quarter of an inch thick, and other things, especially after one end is frequently narrowed to a dull point.

Joss paper: This is a special type of paper used as part of the Chinese funeral ritual to fold the paper representations of a deceased person's money and properties.

Squash: When a flap is separated and flattened. It is not always symmetrically.

Movement arrow: This arrow is put on an origami design to show the direction of the design that the movement of the paper is following.

Noshi: These are special folds of ornamentals with paper that are traditionally attached to gift packages in Japan.

Soft crease: This is a fold that is made carefully so that the crease isn't sharply formed.

Stellated: A star-like origami design.

Frog base: In this base, each flap of a water bomb base is folded at the petals.

Judgement fold: A fold where you cannot locate the point of fold accurately, so you locate it by your eye alone.

Fudge factor: When folding a paper to form a crease, allowance must be made for a small gap to enhance the thickness of the paper.

Modular origami: A modular origami is one where several sheets of paper are folded into different identical modules or units and slotted against each other to form a large geometric design.

Module: This is one element or unit of a whole modular design.

Sonobe unit: This is a unique module that has two flaps and two pockets that can be used to form different shapes.

Grain of paper: Every sheet of paper has a specific direction of grain and it makes it easier to flex along when one axis is compared to the other.

Diagonal fold: This fold involves folding a corner of the opposite corner, creating a sharp diagonal crease.

Skeletal polyhedral: The skeletal polyhedral is a design where the edges of the paper are folded and there are holes on the main face.

Diamond base: This is a base that involves folding two pairs of close edges to a diagonal square having the shape of the diamond.

Painting with paper: This technique is used to paint a simply styled scene to two different colored sides.

Folding level: There are different classifications of origami models in terms of the folding skill required to fold it. Folding levels are designated at simple, low intermediate, intermediate, high intermediate, complex and super complex.

Sink: This term is used to describe a paper when it is reversed after it has been folded along its four edges.

Dog base: An origami base used to fold animal models. It was designed by a popular origamist John Montroll.

Reference finder: This is a computer program that shows the numerical or algebraic expression for a point's coordinates. It is designed by Robert. This reference finder returns the five best short folding sequences that approximate that point.

Dollar bill fold or money fold: This describes the folding of money for gift purposes.

Money folding: The art of using currency notes to create origami designs.

One crease origami: This is a technique used to create one simple crease on a sheet of paper. It was proposed by a British paper folder named Paul Jackson, who happened to explore the many unusual, surprising results.

Paper plane: This art is common amongst children; it is a specialized type of origami, which can fly.

Reverse fold: A reverse fold is when a flap is folded inside or outside another.

Silver rectangle: This is another name for an A4 rectangle coined by a former British folder named John Cunliffe.

Chapter 3

Tips and Tricks Used in Origami

The tips listed here are very basic. Most of them were gotten from age-long professionals in the field. You can trust that you'll be gaining invaluable secrets to help you have a great start in your journey to professionalism in paper folding.

Origami is a very flexible art that allows you to be creative. Hence, these tips are only here to guide you. You can adopt and expand them while following your impulse to create your own designs from scratch. Below is a list of some of these tips that will enable you to get the most out of the origami craft to make the most incredible project.

- Fold with clean hands: This is not just a hygienic practice for yourself, but a hygienic practice that preserves the health of your paper and help it stay clean. Do not for any reason start paper folding after a tough outdoor work without cleaning your hands. Even if you didn't do any dirty work, sweat mixed with dust could cause a

stain. So, ensure your hands are dry and clean even when you are wet folding.
- Be precise: Don't assume your measurements; that could be your greatest nightmare. Precision and accuracy is one precious skill. In your measurements, calculations, folding and attachment, you must be precisely accurate. Wrong estimations can be more disastrous than helpful, so why not take the pain to ensure you are accurate. If it takes you to retake the measurement, give those few seconds to do it. No one achieves any feat in origami by simply estimating or taking guesses at what is to be done. Accuracy is vital because errors multiply quickly. Instead of taking guesses and making wrong estimates, get a plan to follow to instruct you at what point to fold and what amount of measurement to take. Use scoring tools and the right measuring tool for a sharper accuracy, especially when cutting.
- Do not hurry: Except you are in a competition. There is something hurry does to you when you are practicing a craft; you could become so anxious and mix a step or two. Hurry isn't in any

way good for you as a beginner. Slow down and give yourself plenty of time to finish a model. Yeah, give yourself a lot of time when folding; it could take longer than you think. Although, I also encourage you to time yourself when folding, so you get to monitor your progress as you grow in the art. The longer you practice origami, the shorter time it should take you to finish a project. This is why you are encouraged to practice in your leisure where you would have no cause to hurry and be mentally relaxed. You are to enjoy the process of paper folding; origami is not just about the project but the process to the project. So, next time your adrenaline jumps up when you are trying a project, probably for the first time, you should be able to remind yourself to calm down and get rid of hurry.

- Position your paper rightly: Many paper folders don't know how to position their paper to date; it is a beautiful thing that you will be learning this at the very beginning of your journey. Always endeavor to fold the paper away from you and position it so that you will have an allowance to

stretch and fold. Folding away from you rather than towards you helps you to be more precise.
- Fold accurately: In origami, you might be required to fold from an edge to another edge or from an edge to a crease. Whichever it is, ensure to give an accurate fold. Although, folding from edge to edge is way easier than folding from edge to crease.
- When trying a new design, endeavor to use a larger sheet than usual. This will give you more chances for mistakes that you can easily correct. Don't worry about the paper getting rough and unattractive. As a beginner, I'll encourage you to work with a scrapbook, or anything that allows you to make mistakes freely. However, this instruction is only to be followed when you are practicing. If you get stuck while following a diagram to make a new project, refold with a new sheet. You won't want to decorate your house with rumpled sheets.
- If you are planning on majoring in folding with adhesives, you should get a staple gun. It is a handy alternative to glue and a more careful means of joining paper to paper. It prevents

unnecessary spillage of glue on the paper and gives you a more focused point of joining.
- When planning to do a new model of your own, make a rough diagram of it with articulate broken down steps on how to achieve it. No matter how enthralling and exciting it appears to be in your head, you can only get it right when you scribble it down and draw a guide to it. You could also forget the whole steps if you are not careful, that is the worst thing that could happen. So you tend to save a lot by simply documenting your idea. Whether crude or abbreviated, do well to document it.
- You don't need anything to start practicing origami ceremonially; you can start practicing right away and put the little you know to use. Don't be afraid to experiment a new model. There will definitely be the anxiety of getting it right, but don't let it get the greater part of you. Take that bold resolve to try out a new model. Really, it is just paper; no one will shoot you for not getting it right.
- Don't beat yourself up when you make a mistake: Every mistake is an opener to a new idea or a

new technique, or a new lesson learned. Don't beat yourself too much for your errors. Only be sensitive to why you had errors and how to avoid them next time. Also, do well to save your mistakes; they may lead you to new and creative ideas. Trust me, the trash can won't miss them one bit.

- When folding a crease, endeavor to flatten your fold very well. Every crease needs to be well flattened for a successful model, except the instructions tell you to make a blunt crease. Most origamists use their fingertips to make a sharp crease by running their fingers over the fold with due pressure. When making a blunt crease, avoid using your fingertips; just run your hands slightly on the surface. If you are using a very thick paper that is hard to crease, you might need to get a bone folder or improvise to something like a metallic ruler that will flatten your fold without damaging your paper.
- Follow the instructions. Every part of the instructions given in origami is important, so read each description carefully and look at each picture closely. If you miss a piece of information,

it could make the model more difficult than it has to be.

- Be patient. Some artists start origami on a particular day and expect to be experts immediately. It doesn't work that way. Unrealistic expectations could take away your enthusiasm to learn. No one accomplishes anything huge just like that. As a beginner, be patient with yourself even as you maintain intentionality about your growth process. Patience should also be applied when you are practicing. Origami is a contemplative and relaxed activity; therefore, you can't just rush through the instructions without thought. Ensure you are in a relaxed state while you practice and give yourself to learning. Trust me, it won't take long before you become a master and possibly a trainer in origami.
- Have fun: Some trainers won't tell you this, but come to think of it, origami is a relaxation craft, so why can't you just have fun while you practice. You know, you don't have to be all serious and stereotypical. You can have fun while folding. Try

new techniques and experiment with creative ideas.
- Stuck up your tool box: Get a lot of paper, large and small sheets alike. Get sheets of different colors and textures. You could also keep in-store magazine and newspaper sheets; you'll definitely need them one day to make some rare creative artworks. Also, get other tools like scissors, scoring tools and paper folding tools handy, so you won't be uncoordinated when you are ready to fold. Keeping them in one place also helps to ensure that they are in good shape.
- You can start with easy models of just 10 or less steps. Your first project doesn't have to be overly impressive. Keep trying all the techniques one after the other. Go for projects that will enable you to practice and master the techniques used in origami. Repetitive practice helps little children learn and allows them to strengthen their fingers and sharpen their proficiency. Allow the child to fold the model over and over again, for as many times as he is willing to. To capture their interest, choose action models in the beginning. You can

introduce geometric projects and decorative pieces later on.
- Ensure that the working environment is peaceful and very comfortable.
- Meet with other origamists: To advance in origami, you can't afford to be an island of yourself. You will need to meet and interact with other origamists, especially the good ones. It is very important to go for professional hangouts and join origami associations if there are any in your location. When you go for professional hangouts, you get to learn and fold with the very best of paper folders. Also, you get to exchange ideas on how to make creative origami models.
- Don't limit yourself; experiment with all forms of origami. I know I have said this before, but let me just really explain it. Experts in paper art state that origami is very rewarding when you try out different origami forms, like tessellations, modular, and others. In as much as it is important to have a focus on origami, it is more important to be versatile as it helps sharpen your skill on a general note.

- As a paper folder, if there is anything you must really work on outside the craft, then that would be neatness. Paper is highly sensitive to dirt, hence asides from your hands, your work area must also be neat.
- Engage in mini-tutorials: If you cannot participate in a physical or online origami conference, you can engage in mini-tutorials and learn more about origami online. There are several vlogs and blogs owned by professionals in origami that teach several origami designs. In case you ever run out of ideas, you can get refreshed from watching these tutorial videos. However, you don't have to wait until you are out of ideas before fueling your idea box. You can practice many complex models made by professionals and learn the techniques they used in folding. You don't have to get it right; what is important is that you learn the techniques used in each model. Pay close attention to every fold and realize its purpose. You can also memorize their methods of folding different parts. Having a model folder will also help you.

- Practice folding of projects with lots of crease patterns and fewer diagrams. Folding with diagrams as a guide doesn't give much insight to design, like learning to fold crease patterns. It shows exactly how paper is allocated, how the points were formed, and how they are all connected together. The hardest part of designing is adding creases between points.
- The only way to get better at origami is to fold carefully and keep at it. This is one life tip that origami teaches. Even though you don't feel like it, keep trying. Even when you fail, try harder and tougher projects, then go back to try the failed project. For no reason should you give up. Learn through your failures and keep trying.
- Give yourself to learning some tiling and tesselations. It will help the precision and quality of your folding. Trying out many techniques will also help you build a larger repertoire of moves and effects.
- Don't be afraid to show your projects to others for criticism and advice. You can get really helpful suggestions that'll make you a better folder. Criticisms don't kill anyone. Although there are

negative criticisms. That shouldn't be your focus. Learn to sift through negative criticisms and take the good from them after discarding the bad without hesitation.

- Be precise: Ensure that your patterns are precisely accurate, determine how many folds you will need to make and at what point, and the result it will give you. Origami can be very techy. One mistake could ruin a devoted time of concentrated efforts. Ensure to create precise patterns for folding; if you can't create one, research about it and follow the guidelines to make your own.
- Follow guidelines: When displaying innovation and creativity, it is easy to ignore the outlined guidelines in a bid to express your innovation and creativity. I am a lover of order and principles. What is the need of stating precise patterns if you won't follow the stated guidelines to achieve it. If you can, follow the guidelines from the measurement to the positioning and the amount of pressure and paper style.

There are two tricks I'll be teaching subsequently. One is the fastest and easiest way to make a crane, and the other is the wet-folding technique.

To make a crane;

1. Fold the paper in half to form a triangle. If the piece of paper you are using has just one colored side only, start with the colored side facing up. Then unfold the paper and repeatedly make the folds.
2. Now, fold all the creases to form a square with the upper end facing you.
3. Fold two edges in to form a kite shape on top of the paper. Repeat it on the other side
4. Turn the paper to the other side so the colored part is facing down and fold the paper in half till it forms a rectangle. Unfold the folded piece of paper and repeat to make the folds visible.
5. Fold the middle points down and crease above the other two folds. Flip the paper to the other creased side and repeat fold.
6. Go ahead to undo all the folds you made in steps 4 and 5.

7. Pull up the bottom corner till it's up above the top corner. Then fold along the creases you made earlier in steps 4 and 5. Fold it on both sides.
8. Fold two side edges in to form a kite-shape. Repeat on the other side.
9. Fold the top layer of the right side and lay it on top of the left side like you're turning the page of a book. Flip it over and repeat folding on the other side.
10. Fold up the top layer on each side.
11. Repeat the last two steps and fold down the wings on both sides.
12. Bend the head down to give the crane a long and straight beak. Pull the wings straight apart from the body so that the body inflates.

There you have your crane!

Wet-folding;

Wet-folding is a technique used majorly to fold 3D models and projects with round edges. You don't make sharp creases in wet-folding like in other projects. When bending, use the pads of your fingers instead of your fingertips.

Make most of your fold in the air, without tables, to avoid flattening the model during the fold.

If your paper gets dry and stiffen during folding, use the cloth or spray-bottle to add some moisture, but try to do it moderately, so you don't get the paper soaked. After wetting the fold, you start the molding process of bringing your paper to shape.

To enable the mold to dry quickly and retain its shape permanently, use a paper clip or rubber band to keep it in place. A project will be displayed in the coming chapter using the wet folding technique to give you a perfect understanding.

A Short message from the Author:

Hey, I hope you are enjoying the book? I would love to hear your thoughts!

Many readers do not know how hard reviews are to come by and how much they help an author.

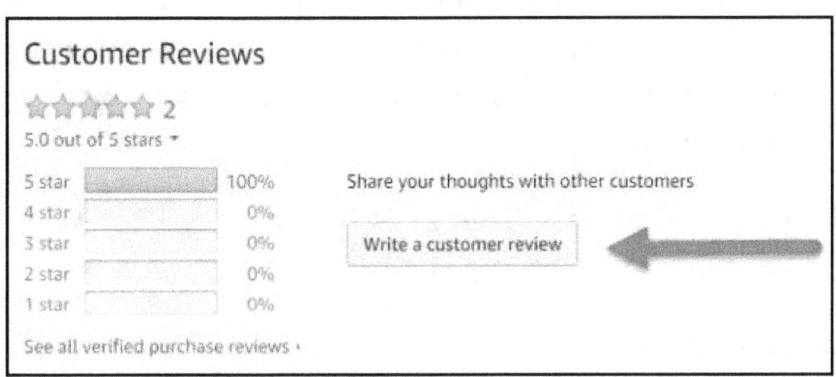

I would be incredibly grateful if you could take just 60 seconds to write a short review on Amazon, even if it is a few sentences!

\>> Click here to leave a quick review

Thanks for the time taken to share your thoughts!

Chapter 4

Getting Started with Origami

In this chapter, I will be discussing the necessary tools needed to make your first origami project and the basic techniques required; some of them have been mentioned in the previous chapters. They will only be explained more extensively here.

Tools and Materials Used in Origami

Origami Paper

Any flat material can be used for folding, but not all papers can be used in certain origami projects. The major qualification of an origami paper is any paper that can hold a crease. There are different types of origami paper; some are double-colored, some with color on one side, and others are plain white papers. Although some persons use copy paper in place of origami paper, origami paper is more advisable and malleable for any origami project you intend to do. Usually, copy paper weighs more than origami paper.

Normal copy paper weighs between 70-90 cm. These papers can be used for simple folds, such as crane and waterbomb. It is hardly ever used for major folding in origami. Heavy origami papers are used for technical projects that involve techniques like wet folding.

Unryu, lokta, hanji, gampi and abaca are artisan papers that have long, strong fibers. These papers are floppy and are often back coated with methylcellulose or wheat paste before folding. The papers are thin and easily compressible; hence the back coat helps retain a little stability. They are majorly used in making thin origami models like insect models. Paper money from various countries is also popularly used such as Dollar money, Orikane, and Money Origami.

If you want to achieve certain origami projects, there are certain types of paper that you use. For most origami projects, you can't just use copy/printer paper or craft paper to make origami projects.

Paper texture and color is one thing that you must consider when folding origami. You will want to get paper that can be folded and won't unfold after it has been crafted into a design, a base, or a paper that won't crack after it has been folded. Some paper production companies, especially in Japan, use non-toxic, long-lasting inks that fill the papers' cracks to give a smooth surface when folded. Also, the thickness of the paper determines the kind of models that can be folded with it. Thin paper is most flexible and can be folded into any shape you desire. Below is a list of various kinds of origami paper.

Types of origami paper

1. Standard Origami paper, also called Kami

This is by all ramifications the best paper for most origami projects. This paper was introduced by Japan and is still being produced by Japan. One of the features of Kami is that it has color on just one side of the paper; the other side is plain white. Although, there are kami papers that are without color. They are 0.66 millimeters, unlike the dyed paper, which is 0.71 mm thick.

There are about 60 different color options for Kami paper; another reason why it is a better choice to use for Origami. It varies in size: length and width.

Kami paper is known to hold creases very well, and it is proven to be one of the easiest papers to use.

Care to know another bumper reason why you should get this paper? It is very affordable and is widely available. You don't need to comb all your local stores for a box of kami sheets. Here you have it, the best and most malleable origami paper-kami.

2. TANT paper

It won't be out of place to put this origami paper next to Kami. It is a very fine and attractive paper for origami décor ideas. It has a beautiful patterned texture and a nice sheen on the surface. For many folders, it is the texture that attracts them to this paper. Same for me.

Tant paper is 1.18 mm thick; it is generally thicker than other sheets.

Another fact to interest you is that Tant's name means a lot, that is, abundance of colors. It is mostly famous in Japan because of its beautiful texture that remains unbreakable despite the number of creases you make with it. This paper is however more expensive than the Kami paper and is used majorly for décor. You should use this for your interior or ceremonial décor. It will upgrade the look of your origami projects.

3. Duo color standard paper

From the name, you can guess rightly how this paper looks. The duo color standard paper has both sides colored with ink. Sometimes, it is the same color, other times, it could be two different colors at the front and back. The application of the colored ink on both sides of the paper makes it more expensive because of the added cost of ink. The extra color on it also increases the thickness of the paper. The thickness of a duo standard paper is estimated at 0.76mm. It is popularly made in China.

4. Washi

It has a unique Japanese feel and look. Ancient Japanese folders invented it; hence it was the most commonly used paper for a very long time. The texture of this paper is fabric-like and very soft when felt. The washi paper comes in 50 different multicolored packs. This sheet is very thick, far thicker than the two standard sheets. It is measured at 0.94mm. However, it is very durable and the perfect paper for the wet-folding technique. This is a great choice for projects you want to keep for a long time; you can trust Washi paper for durability. Models made using washi paper usually appear more real because of their soft fabric-like texture. Varied in sizes, the washi paper has very long fibers that help it maintain shape after it is folded. One downside of this ancient paper is that it is available only in basic colors.

5. Tissue foil paper

An amazing and easy to fold paper for beginners in origami. It is made of foil and tissue, as the name depicts. An interesting combination that makes the paper stiff and slightly flexible at the same time. It provides a wide variety of color types with a particular color on both sides of the paper. Unlike the Duo color stand paper, this paper is relatively thin and can come in very large sheets. There are also a variety of textures you have to select from. It holds creases very well and is well malleable. However, it doesn't give room for mistakes and could easily get damaged. Talk about the price of quality ; this paper is the most expensive.

Asides from the origami paper, there are other materials used in origami projects. Yeah, I know I mentioned that traditional origami was just paper and your two hands, but with many creative models, other simple materials can be used in Origami. Some of these materials are a must-have for complex origami projects. Worry not; there are just a few of them. Nothing complex! Origami is still that simple and creative art it has always been.

Below are the five extra tools you should consider adding to your kit for origami.

Paper Folding Tool

The number one folding tool is your hands, but you can't use your hands for all models. There are some technical folds you can only achieve with a paper folding tool. This tool is also used when you have several models to fold. The importance of a paper model is to help flatten the fold smoothly without giving room for unnecessary puffs. These tools have taken the place of fingernails in the folding exercise. It is more effective and efficient. For many years, the most popular folding tool used in origami is the bone folder. Traditionally this tool was simply made from an animal's bone. That is how it earned the name.

However, today there are many modern types of bone folders; some are made of plastic, metal, or wood. You can get them from any local craft store around you. In place of a bone folder, you can improvise with a plastic knife, letter opener, or clay shaping tools. Any improvising tool you will use must be something that is easy to hold and knife-shaped with a blunt edge.

Scoring Tool

The scoring tool is used to score a clean line on your paper to make a fold without causing damage to the paper. There are several scoring tools in craft supply stores, but it is not a must that you must purchase one when you could simply improvise and get the same result. All you need is to look out for a straight and smooth-edged item that you can use to make a score and mark a perfect point to make a fold.

You can consider using an empty cased ballpoint pen, a blunt butter knife, a metal ruler, or a knitting needle in a pinch. To make a score, place your ruler on the particular place where the fold should be, then drag your scoring tool along the ruler as though you are drawing a line, but make sure you mark a slight mark to avoid tearing the paper apart. Scoring tools are necessary when trying complex projects, using a big thick paper or expensive paper.

You won't want to condemn an expensive quality paper like tissue foil because of a mistake during folding that could have been avoided. Hence, a scoring tool's major advantage is that it prevents you from having many damages and enables you to fold on a straight line.

Glue

Some origami projects require the use of adhesives to keep them perfectly in place. There are complex projects that are done with thick paper. You cannot use glue on light paper; it will not go well at all. Hence, you must be sure your project needs a glue before applying one; don't be in a hurry to jump and apply glue when you could easily hold your fold down by flattening it with a bone folder. You will see some of the unique projects that require glue in the coming chapter.

It is majorly used in joining multiple modules together to create a 3D piece of origami art. It is also handy for attaching your origami model to a picture frame or a greeting card. For those who are glue-averse, you can use a double-sided tape; it gives just the same result.

Ruler

For accuracy, you will have to measure your paper and determine where each fold will be and what length you will make the model. The metallic and stainless steel rulers are the most commonly used ruler in origami.

Scissors

There are several cutting tools; all of them are manual and simple to use. The simplest and oldest cutting tool is the scissors. After making your measurement or drawing the shape of the design you want to make on paper, you'll need to cut out the excess paper. This is where the scissors come in. It is simple and easy to maneuver the scissors round a paper and make a perfect cut.

It is also used to make paper divisions after deciding the size of paper you want to use for your project. Also, it is very portable and mobile-friendly. When purchasing scissors, ensure it is very sharp as blunt scissors could do you more harm than good. Asides from the ancient scissors, another cutting tool is the paper trimmer. This one is quite mechanical and comes with a ruler to ensure you make that perfect cut without giving your paper unnecessary marks.

Paper Clips

This is a must-have when you are making a lot of technical projects at the same time. It is a colored plastic used in holding paper down while you work on another side of the paper, or it can be used to hold a design down during final assembly. I don't know of any improvised alternative. It is paper clips or paper clips.

Basic Origami Folding Symbols

There are several origami folding symbols. These symbols are represented in the picture diagram below. It is essential you know these symbols because you will encounter them more often in your practice of origami. Some tutorials might not give you the step by step guide to making projects; they might represent the steps in illustrative diagrams using these symbols. Thus, it is highly imperative that you learn these symbols and what they represent.

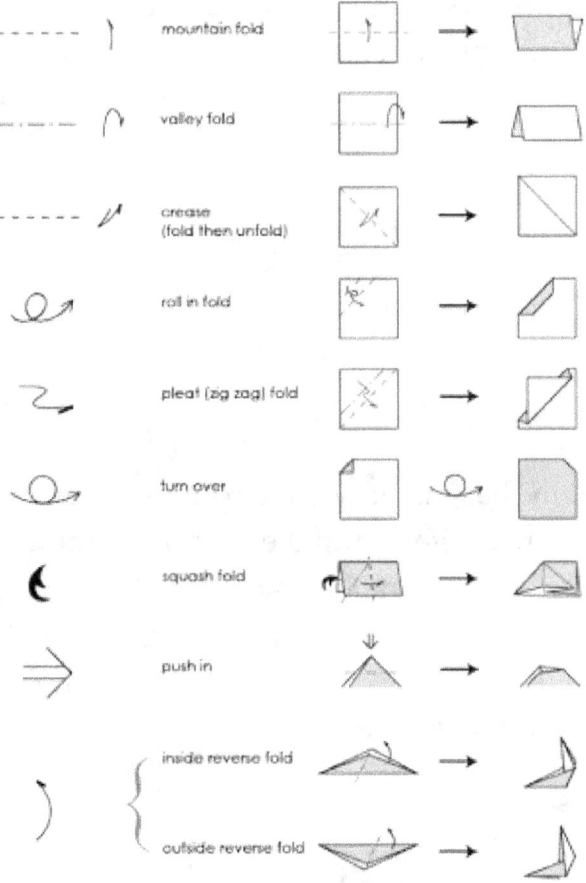

Common Origami Bases

Bases are a short series of folds that can be developed into a variety of styles and folds. The most common bases that are first learnt in origami are bird and water bomb bases. Most models are made from these bases.

Kite Bases

This origami base is very easy to make, but you cannot fly it like a real kite. To make this base, rotate a square sheet of paper diagonally, fold it, make a sharp crease, and then unfold it. Fold the lower edges of both sides to the center so that they can touch each other, and you will have your kite base.

Blintz Bases

This base is named after the blintz pancake. Place your square sheet of paper in a straight position and fold it in half. Unfold it and fold the paper from left to right. Unfold the paper and place it diagonally. There you have the blitz base.

Preliminary Base

Position your square sheet of paper properly and fold the paper from left to right. Sharpen the crease and fold the paper in the middle. Fold the right corner so that it touches the middle. Fold the left corner so that the two corners form a triangle. Open the bottom of the triangle by lifting the center. Open it until it collapses into a square. Rotate the square until it shows the shape of a diamond.

Water Bomb Base

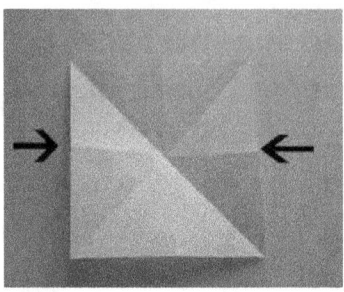

This is another commonly used base. To make this base, fold the paper in half diagonally, so that it forms the shape of a triangle. Then fold the triangle into two and unfold it.

Fish Base

The fish base is a starting point to make unique fish models. Rotate the sheet of origami paper diagonally and fold it in half. Unfold it, and fold the paper from left to right. Then unfold it so that the paper has a cross shape. Fold the left and right corners to the middle to give you a preliminary base. Turn the paper upside down. Fold the bottom point to the top point. Turn the paper to the other side and open the fold. Fold down the left flap, crease the inside corner, do the same to the right flap. Fold the layer back down to make it a perfect fish base.

Windmill Base

The windmill base is not as common as other bases, but it is used majorly to make a star. Fold a rectangular paper in half, unfold it, and fold the top part so that it touches the middle crease. Fold the bottom part too so it touches the crease, then fold it in half so that the left touches the right. Unfold and fold the left paper so it touches the middle crease. Make a triangle shape on the left flap. Fold the flap down. Fold the right edge to the center, told the corners that flap the middle. Pull out the bottom of the layer and complete the base until it looks like what you have above.

Bird Base

Here we have another popular base. Fold the paper to form a preliminary base. Then fold the bottom left and right edges. Fold the top triangle down on top of the paper. Then unfold all three flaps. Open the top-bottom layer, lift it up while folding in the sides, and turn the paper back. Fold the left and edges to the center. Fold the thick triangle down again and unfold all three flaps. Lift the bottom up and open. Fold down the two flaps at the front and back. The base is done.

Basic Origami Folds

These are common folds you are certain to come across in your practice of origami. A model could be made with one or more of these folds. A diagram has been added to each of these folds to give you an idea of how yours should be when practicing.

Valley Folds

Valley folds are achieved by joining two points of the same paper together and folding it in half. The result is that the crease is down, and the folds go up.

Mountain Folds

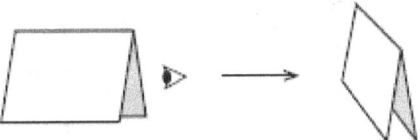

This is the exact opposite of the valley folds. The vertex goes up and the folds go down.

Double folding is having the two folds; valley and mountain, fold in one project.

Inside Reverse Fold

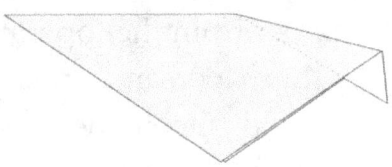

This is a form of fold where the paper is folded into the model. The paper is placed at angle 45 and folded diagonally. Fold the right end of your folded paper.

Crease it well and unfold it. Turn the paper over and make a sharp fold, crease and unfold it. Push the paper from the just unfolded side into the paper. Push the fold into the paper until all of it is inside.

Outside Reverse Fold

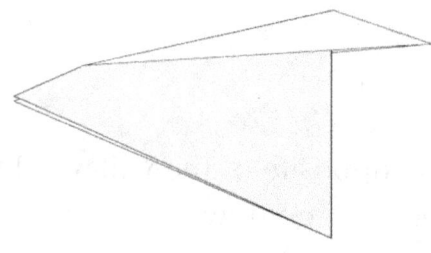

This fold is the opposite of the inside reverse fold. To achieve this, get a paper and fold it diagonally. Make a valley fold on the paper from the top paper. Crease and unfold. Turn over the paper and make another valley fold. Crease and unfold. Open the model and fold it down. Make a mountain fold and close the paper again.

Rabbit Ear Fold

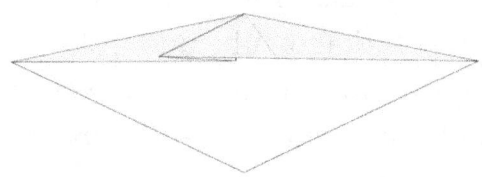

Make a sharp crease on a square paper, diagonally on a square paper and unfold it, then fold the upper right part of the paper so that it aligns with the crease, unfold and do the same with the upper left part and unfold so that you have an X sign above the crease. Then try joining the two upper sides together, don't place them against each other; let their sides touch. It will give you a sharp pointed mouth, bend that mouth to the side; you have your rabbit ear already.

Squash Fold

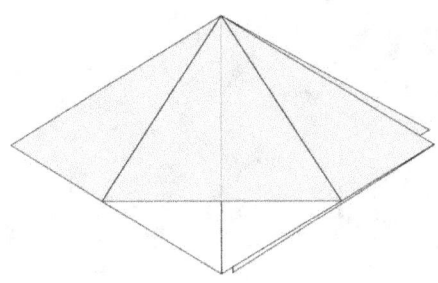

You can make a squash fold with any shape of paper. Place your paper diagonally and fold it on the two sides. It will give you a cone-like shape. Flatten it down to make it look like what you have above. Ensure that both sides are symmetrical.

Pleat

This fold is done with a simple rectangle-shaped sheet. Fold the left side of the paper to the back, then fold the right side to the left.

Sink Fold

Make a waterbomb base, fold the tip of the triangle and unfold it. Make sure the fold is average; it shouldn't be too long or short. Then open up the triangle. Then you flatten the top so that it resembles a table, then manipulate the crease sides of the triangle so that it comes to the center while you are sinking in.

Chapter 5

Origami Project Ideas

Here we are already, ready to try our hands on something. Trust me; origami is one of the simplest things you'll ever try doing asides from eating. Many of the origami projects listed here are quite ancient and can be traced far back to several years ago. Isn't that thrilling? Yeah, I thought it lovely to take you down the trail to the time when origami was a cherished cultural art. You might probably be inspired by the ancient project and get motivated to try out modern and complex origami projects. The projects we will be discussing are simple, with steps you can easily remember.

Most of these projects are amazing interior and exterior décor; others are simply fun ideas you can teach a kid or use as a gift item to surprise your loved ones. They are all durable beautiful pieces everyone will love to own.

Listed here are 25 interesting projects you can do as a beginner. These awesome craft ideas are for both adults, teenagers, and children alike.

So, here we go!

DIY Crane Garland

Tropical countries commonly use a Crane Garland to welcome guests or give a salute to a graduating student. It is not really a ceremonial thing but a good decor to consider for a welcome party as it is used in many parts of the world. If you have an outdoor party, you should consider using this as a decor.

Supplies

- Origami paper
- Scissors
- Perfect thread
- Plier

Procedures

Step 1: Follow the instructions in the previous chapter to fold origami paper into cranes.

Step 2: String the wire into the eye of a needle, thread it from the top of the crane. Then, pull from the top of the crane through the bottom.

Step 3. Thread a ring onto the wire, continue alternating between stringing cranes, and ring down the wire's length.

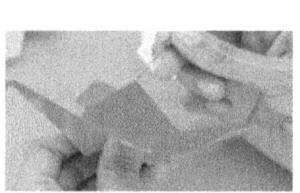 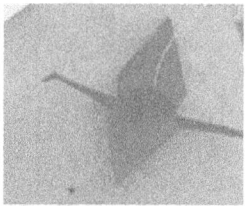

Step 4: Space the cranes out as desired, crimp the rings just beneath the birds to act as stoppers.

Step 5: Repeat to create multiple garlands, then hang them with rod or hooks.

Heart Escort Card

Planning to send a letter to someone you love, this heart escort card is a perfect escort to add to that letter too. I could imagine a smile already on my face if I received such a gift or letter from a loved one or a secret admirer. This is really heartwarming. All you need to make this card is a sheet of plain paper. You could use a colored one if you wish.

Procedures

Step 1: Get a plain square paper and fold it to the shape of a triangle.

Step 2: Loosen the folded triangle and refold it diagonally.

Step 3: Turn the paper over.

Step 4: Unfold the paper and fold the top to the middle.

Step 5: Fold the down part up till it covers the top folded paper.

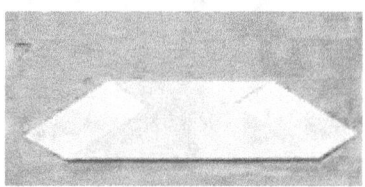

Step 6: Fold the paper in a slant from the right side, as you can see in the image.

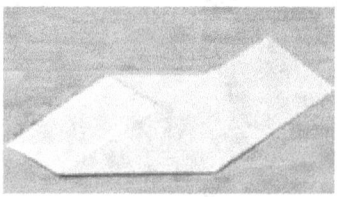

Step 7: Make a similar fold on the left side.

Step 8: Turn your paper to the back and fold the sharp edges at the sides slightly.

Step 9: Fold the sharp top edge also. Turn your paper around again, and there you have it!

Heart Page Marker

Are you a bookworm, or you have a loved one who never gets tired of consuming books? This page keeper is a great gift idea and library collection for all book lovers.

Again, all you need is a square piece of thick paper. You can use cardboard paper.

Procedures

Step 1: Fold in half and crease.

Step 2: Fold in half again and crease.

Step 3: Open up all of the creases.

Step 4: Fold the bottom portion to meet the middle crease line.

Step 5: Turn over and fold up the edges in a triangular shape.

Step 6: Turn over and bring the triangle to the top.

Step 7: Turn over again and use your finger to make an opening from the bottom of the triangle.

Step 8: Flatten it to form a triangle.

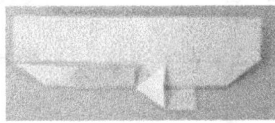

Step 9: Repeat the same step above on the left side.

Step 10: Fold a triangle from the edge for both sides.

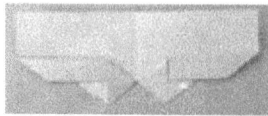

Step 11: Fold a tiny triangle from each peak.

Step 12: Turn over and fold the areas behind the dotted lines and your book page marker is ready.

Butterfly

This simple craft is great to consider are a child or an adult. The steps are basically easy and educating. A fun craft for both children and adults. A beautiful decorative piece.

All you need for this project is a simple square paper and your hands. No need for cuts or adhesives. This is an original origami project.

Procedures

Step 1: Fold your paper in half both ways and unfold.

Step 2: Fold both ways diagonally and unfold.

Step 3: Collapse into a waterbomb base.

Step 4: Fold the upper layer only

Step 5: Turn over and fold the corner past the edge.

Step 6: Fold behind, turn over.

Step 7: Fold along the centerline.

Step 8: Your butterfly is ready.

Heart Origami

Who could have thought a paper can be made to be a heart that is perfect in shape and perfect in form? This heart looks so solid and beautiful; you can hang it in your apartment with thread or simply leave it lying on your reading table. To make this beautiful piece, you need thick rectangular paper and scissors.

Procedures

Step 1: Fold the paper in half to make a sharp crease at the middle and unfold it.

Step 2: Refold the paper again and fold it in half to make a sharp crease.

Step 3: Unfold and fold both edges to make a triangular shape, but don't make a sharp tip. The two edges mustn't touch.

Step 4: Fold the two bottom sides of the triangle up.

Step 5: Unfold it and close the edges of the triangle.

Step 6: Lift the bottom edges and pull the inner paper out.

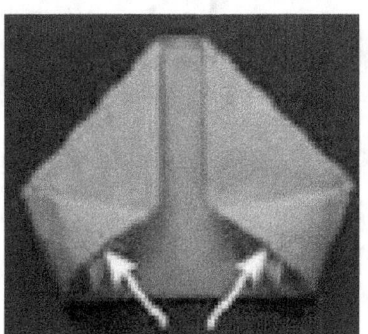

Step 7: Turn the paper over and push the top inside to form the middle of a heart.

Step 8: Adjust the bottom until you get this perfect shape.

Halloween Design

Worried about the right design to make for your Halloween décor that will give you that horror and bloody look? Here is a project you can try. With just a sheet of red and white paper, you can make a real Halloween design and bring the spirit of Halloween to life.

Procedures

Step 1: Place the white side of the paper up, crease diagonally and unfold.

Step 2: Now, you are going to make a lot of creases. Fold the corners to the center and crease. Fold the new corners to the center, crease and unfold. Fold the bottom and the top to the center line and unfold. Unfold the right and left flaps. Then fold the bottom up to the center again. Make another fold with the right flap so that it touches the top corner.

Step 3: Lower the right and left flap and flatten.

Step 4: Open all center flaps and fold the top downwards so that it touches the center. Lift the right sharp flap, spread it out and flatten it lightly into a diamond shape. Repeat the same with the other side.

Step 5: Fold the two edges towards the center of each diamond. Pinch out the center of the white part, then fold it together. Ensure the edges flat while folding it downward. It is supposed to give you a fang. Repeat on the other side.

Step 6: Open the two flaps and tuck in the white parts so that only the fangs are visible. Then fold the model in half and fold back the top point. Your project is done!

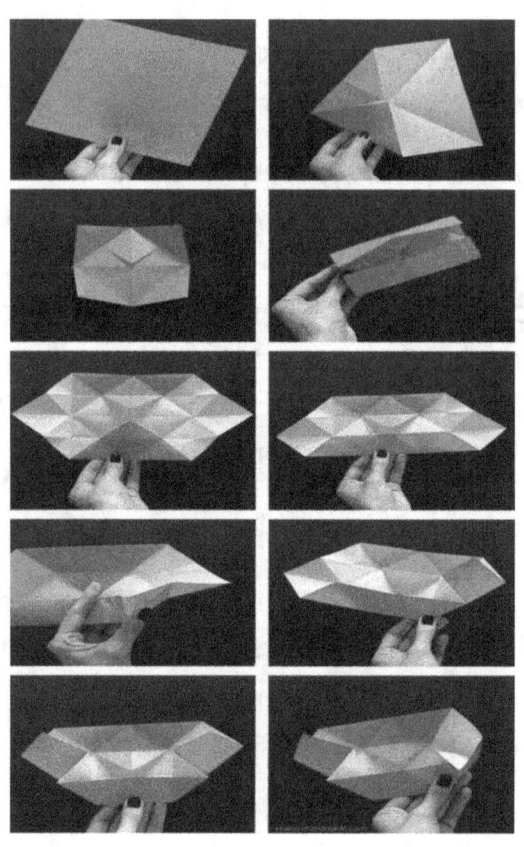

Paper Star

This is one very attractive and simple project you will love to try out. You can use any paper to make this project. Paper stars are also basic projects little children will be interested in.

Procedures

Step 1: Fold your square diagonally.

Step 2: Make a kite base

Step 3: Unfold the kite base and fold the two top corners into a triangle. Fold the lower corners over it to form a kite shape.

Step 4: Fold the top triangle over the lower one slightly.

Step 5: Turn it over and make a sharp crease at that point.

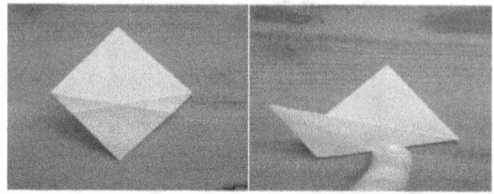

Step 6: Turn over and lift the triangles up so they look like this.

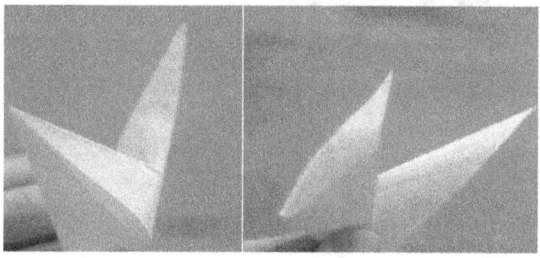

Step 7: Open the bottom of the fold as wide as you can.

Step 8: Create as many as you can but don't make so much, so you can have a perfect star and they can all easily join together.

Step 9: Join the paper folds together by placing the paper over each other. Here you have your paper star.

Origami Boat

Asides from paper plane, this is one other simple craft children love to make just for fun. They find it very entertaining and interesting. If you wish, you can create a chain of these paper boats and hang them on your child's room wall or in your classroom. You don't need any adhesives; a colorful square paper is all you need.

Procedures

Step 1: First, form a triangle with the top corners.

Step 2: Then twist one side of the triangle.

Step 3: Twist the corners to the other side.

Step 4: Gently unfold the corners until you have a well-made boat.

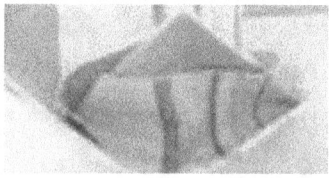

If you wish to create a thread of origami boats, get a colored thread and pass it through a needle.

Then pass it through the middle tip of the boat. Following this sequence, thread as many boats as you have made.

Origami Lampstand

This lampstand is exquisitely beautiful and very attractive. You can place this in the center of your living room. Trust me, people are going to want to inquire where you got this lampstand from. You can make it as a gift for your loved one.

Procedures

Step 1: Cut out a rectangular piece on the wallpaper.

Step 2: Thread the top of the wallpaper together in a spaced manner, like in the image below.

Step 3: Thread the bottom of the wallpaper together and tie it together.

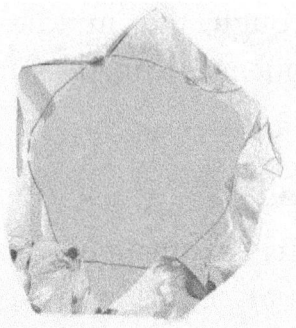

Step 4: String the thread tightly to ensure the shade folds in the right places. Don't tie it up yet; you will still need to adjust it when you pass the flex and bulb through the top of the shade.

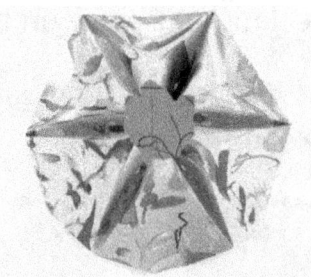

Step 5: Insert the flex through the top of the shade, and then screw in a cold bulb. Do not use a hot bulb as it can burn the lampstand. You can now tighten the thread around the lamp.

Lotus Flower

A lotus flower is a very beautiful flower known as a symbol of purity and beauty. In the age-long cartoon "Avatar, The Legend of Ang," a white lotus was used as the representation of identity for the people who seek philosophy, beauty and truth. In many places like China, it is still reverenced as a symbol of purity. To make this flower, you will need two different paper colors; green and any other color of your choice. Your paper must be rectangular in shape.

Procedures

Step 1: Fold your paper in half and make a sharp crease.

Step 2: Unfold it and fold the two corners to form a short triangle.

Step 3: Fold the top and bottom sides over the triangle.

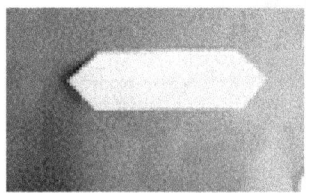 

Step 4: Repeat steps one to three to all the number of papers you intend to use in making the lotus flower. I suggest four folds of each color.

Step 5: Join all the paper folds of one color together in a star-like manner. Use paper pins to hold them in place.

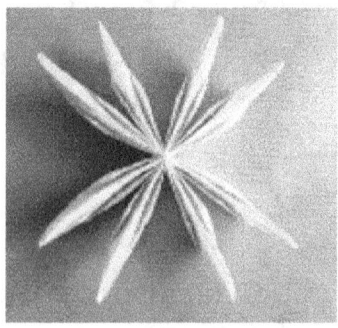

Step 6: Start spreading out the folds, so that it is curved upwards.

Step 7: Join the paper folds of the other colors together also and hold them in place.

Step 8: Curve it up slightly without spreading it out.

Step 9: Place the spread folds on top of the other curved fold. Your lotus flower is ready for display.

DIY Ice Cream Origami

You'll agree with me that this ice cream cone looks so real and amazing. Like you could want to eat it already even though it isn't real. A very creative and interesting craft that you should try.

Procedures

Step 1: Black coat two of your chosen colors together. If you can get a piece of paper with two colors, you'll not need to black coat.

Step 2: Fold it diagonally, create a sharp crease and unfold.

Step 3: Make a kite base

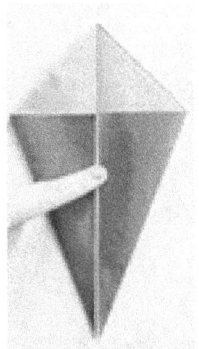

Step 4: Pull the sides of the triangle apart.

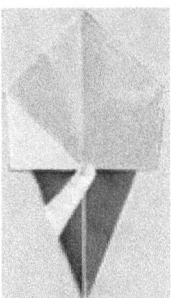

Step 5: Turnover and fold the sides you pulled gently so that it touches the back.

Step 6: Form a triangle

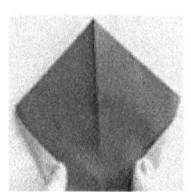 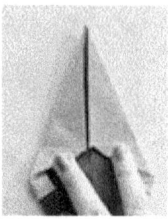

Step 7: Fold the triangle to create a pleat.

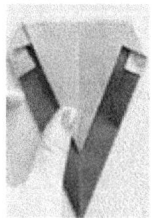

Step 8: Continue folding until you have at least three pleats. You can use your scissors to cut small circles of different colors of paper and glue them to the top pleated part of your icecream.

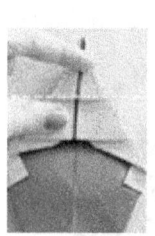 

Pencil Holder

The pencil holder is a great tool to have if you're packing your bag for a journey. A pencil holder will help the organization of your bag's things and help you avoid messing things up and ruining the other stuff you have packed in your bag. It is also a perfect project for you if you are a beginner.

Procedures

Step 1: Cut your origami paper to size according to the size of your pencils.

Step 2: Fold your square paper in half with the pattern facing down.

Step 3: Turn your paper to the back and fold all the sides to meet the centerfold.

Step 4: Open out the sides out and fold the top left corner so that it meets the centerfold.

Step 5: Fold the top right corner of the sheet to meet the 1st fold from the right.

Step 6: Fold the right side to the center and then the left-hand side over to the right.

Step 7: Wrap the last flap around to the back. You can use a little glue to place the back flap.

Step 8: Flip your sheet of paper to the other side and slide your pencils into the pocket.

Your pencil holder is ready.

Paper Flower

This ambient flower is a beautiful interior decor. I can imagine this on a shelf or center table; its beauty is enthralling and captivating. Also very simple to make. It involves very direct and clear steps. You can try this out with the following tools.

Supplies

- A pencil or scalpel
- A cardboard paper or TANT paper
- Flexible metal wire or rod
- A scissors
- Floral green ribbon
- Glue

Procedures

Step 1: Cut a rectangle of cardboard and fold it in half.

Step 2: We draw the leaves with a scalpel or pencil

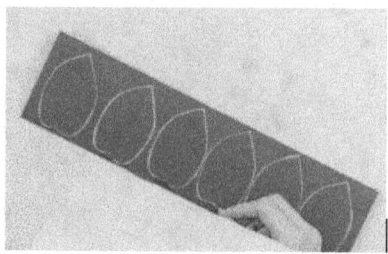

Step 3: Make a small cut in the lower part to introduce the floral wire.

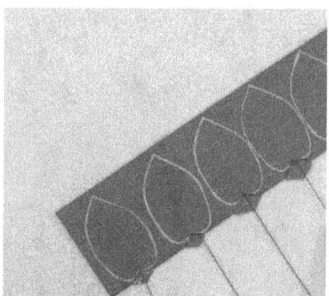

Step 4: Cut the leaves out with scissors and open the paper to apply glue so that the wire can stick well to the leaf.

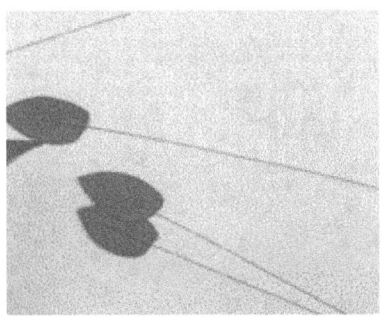

Step 5: Cover the wire with floral tape and make holes in the leaves with a scalpel or cutter.

Step 6: Get your polystyrene ready.

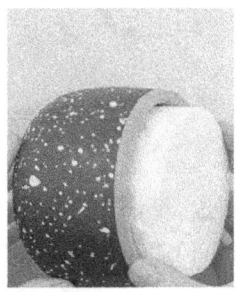

Step 7: Begin to mark where you are going to put your flowers.

Step 8: Finally, insert all of your flowers into the polystyrene, and now we have our beautiful paper flowers.

Paper Clutch

This paper clutch is classic and chic. You'll be surprised it involves just a few steps to make.

Supplies

- A colored cardboard 31 x 31 cm
- Adhesive book cover 33 x 75 cm approx.
- Scissors
- Pencil
- Rule
- Glue stick

Procedures

Step 1: Mark the center using a ruler and join the lateral vertices to the middle.

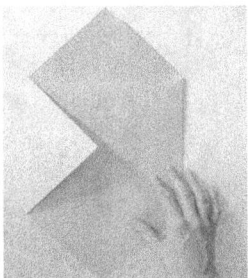

Step 2: Mark with the pencil the line where we should fold the upper flap. Fold the lower flap so that it touches that mark you made.

Step 3: Unfold the flap and fold the lower vertex back to the crease just made.

Step 4: Fold the sides so that it stays on top of the folded part.

Step 5: Make a square at the bottom vertex.

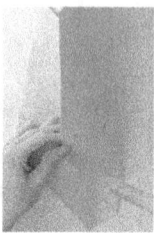

Step 6: Unfold and fold the lower vertex.

Step 7: Raise the square as follows

Step 8: Fold back in the middle of the square.

Step 9: Unfold and change the direction of the fold so that the flaps on the sides can easily be pulled over the bottom flap.

Step 10: Bring the upper vertex to the lower horizontal side. Unfold and fold back to the mark we made in step 2.

Flower Vase

This is one of the most amazing origami projects you will certainly fall in love with. A modern and sleek vase everyone will love to have. You can place it on the shelf or table. This model is very elegant and easy to make.

Supplies

- Paper in the color of your choice
- Bread knife/ bone folder
- Pencil
- Scissors
- Ruler
- Glue stick

Procedures

Step 1: First, cut a rectangle out of construction paper

Step 2: Divide the rectangle into 6 cm wide strips. The extra sides will be used as flaps later on.

Step 3: Turn over and connect the upper left corner as shown below

Step 4: Now, connect the corner at the bottom left with the top's 2nd mark.

Step 5: Repeat with the remaining markings. Run the knife and ruler along all the lines so that the marked line gives a sharp edge.

Step 6: Then fold along all the lines to get sharper edges, fold and press it well so that the edges get really sharp.

Step 7: Then rule a line at the two edges, smear adhesive flap and fasten the two ends together.

Step 8: It should have a square shape at the beginning and end.

Christmas Tree Décor

Do you have a mesmerizing love for the colorful lanterns people put on a Christmas tree? You'll be learning how to make yours in this tutorial. I can feel the excitement of having this on my Christmas tree or on my walls. It is such a beauty coming from you already. Let's get to it already.

To get started, you need to get the following tools;

- A4 Paper
- Scissors
- Ruler
- Needle (for scoring)
- Double-sided tape/glue
- Printable templates

Procedures

Step 1: Print the 'Model A' template on the A4 paper. Cut out the template.

Step 2: Score all the dotted lines using a ruler and compass.

Step 3: Pass the needle through all of the endpoints of the line along either side of the template.

Step 4: Fold along all the horizontal lines as shown in the diagram below.

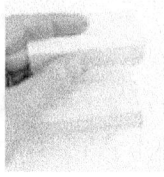

Step 5: Flip the paper over and press in the central zig-zag.

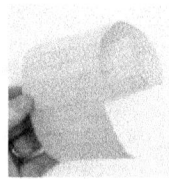

Step 6: Slowly collapse the paper.

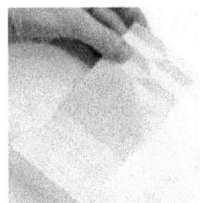

Step 7: Continue collapsing the paper until the end of the strip.

Step 8: String some thread through the holes and run along one side of the piece of paper, except the first and last holes. Repeat on the other side of the paper.

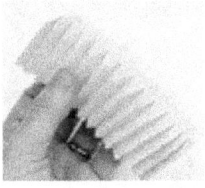

Step 9: Flatten the strip of paper at both ends.

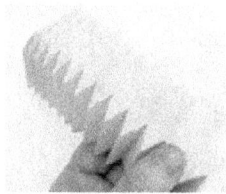

Step 10: Bring the two ends together and glue them into position.

Step 11: Sew the thread through the remaining holes and pull it tight, then tie.

Butterflies

This beautiful butterfly is very creative and artistic one. A perfect project to hone your creativity and work with your imagination. All you need is a square of paper of any size, pattern or type will do. You can create four butterflies from one sheet of A4 plain paper with the following steps.

Procedures

Step 1: Place your A4 sheet of plain paper horizontally, and fold the paper, so the bottom left-hand corner meets with the top of the paper

Step 2: Remove the excess paper on the right-hand side to produce your square

Step 3: Fold the paper in half on the diagonal, horizontal and vertical, to mark the square

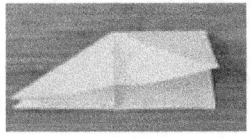

Step 4: Cut the square paper into four along the horizontal and vertical lines

Step 5: Repeat the diagonal, horizontal and vertical folds on each square. You can represent the sides with letters.

Corner A = Top Left

Corner B = Top Right

Corner C = Bottom Left

Corner D = Bottom Right

Step 6: Place the squares straight, bring corner (A) to meet corner (D)

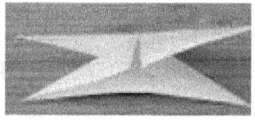

Step 7: Keeping the center fold lines in place, bring corner (A) back to meet the corner (C) so that you form a triangle fold on the left side.

Step 8: Repeat this on the opposite side to create a complete triangle fold.

Step 9: Fold corner A across the vertical centerline.

Step 10: Repeat this along the right side.

Step 11: Turn the triangle over so that the top point is facing you. Bend the top layer well so that it overlaps the bottom of the triangle.

Step 12: Secure it in place by folding the tip of the triangle over the bottom line.

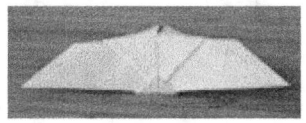

Step 13: Finally, fold it in half across the bottom of the triangle and press down the fold.

Your butterfly is ready.

Envelope

One benefit of origami is it allows you to make the most attractive pieces with scrap. Without glue or adhesives, you can make this lovely envelope to send a memo or letter to a friend. You can also use it to make a store some paper files.

All you need to make this beautiful piece is a scrapbook and ruler.

Procedures

Step 1: Fold your paper in half on the diagonal to form a triangle.

Step 2: Take the top layer and fold it down to the bottom edge of your triangle.

Step 3: Use your ruler to a third of your scrapbook; take the right corner of your triangle, and fold it into your 1/3 mark.

Step 4: Next, take your left corner and fold it to the edge of the right-hand side. Flatten it with your hands and crease. Ensure you have a smooth and straight crease.

Step 5: Fold the top flap you just folded back on itself. Make the corner of the triangle touch the edge of the left-hand side.

Step 6: Unfold and open the fold. Flatten the fold to form a diamond-shaped pocket.

Candy Purse

This heart-shaped candy is very attractive and cool. You can teach this to a kid, so they store their candy on the shelf properly. If you own a local store, you could also make this solid candy box to store your candy. It also makes a good gift to a candy lover on valentine's day.

All you need are three squared paper and double-sided tape. You can also use a bone folder for crisp folds.

Procedures

Steps 1: Fold one square in half diagonally.

Steps 2: Fold each corner down to meet the bottom corner. Crease and unfold.

Steps 3: Fold the bottom corners up so that it touches the center. Crease and unfold.

Steps 4: Repeat these folds with the other two paper squares.

Steps 5: Join the three pieces by sliding one corner into another.

Steps 6: Connect the two ends by sliding the corner into each other the same way you did in the last step.

Making sure the bottom flaps are alternate so the bottom won't fall out.

Steps 7: You can add a small piece of double-sided tape to the bottom flaps to make it more secure.

Kusudama Flower

And here is yet another paper flower design, which are popular decorations used during holidays and parties. It can come in a variety of colors and shapes. This is a nice DIY project to make an origami paper flower ball. It was innovated in Japan and is also called kusudama. It is usually created by or gluing multiple identical pyramid-shaped units together to form a spherical shape.

Supplies

- Colored paper

- Glue
- Sharp pencil
- Scissors

Procedures

Step 1: Get rectangular papers of different colors.

Step 2: Make a bird base

Step 3: Fold the bird base in half from the middle point.

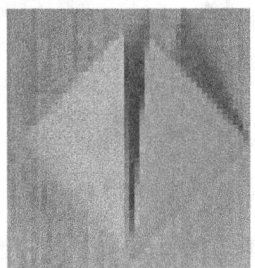

Step 4: Open the flaps and spread them out.

Step 5: Fold the corner of the flaps slightly

Step 6: Pleat the sides of the pleat and bring the edges together. You can add a little glue to make it sturdy.

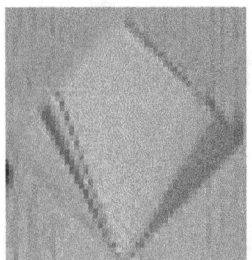 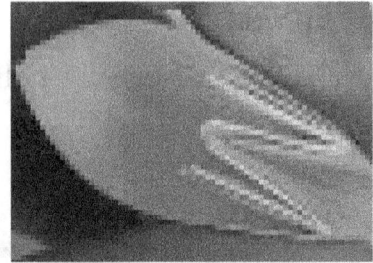

Step 7: Repeat the process and make four more folds to make a flower.

Step 8: Join the folds together with glue.

You can make more flowers if you wish to.

Origami Roses

This origami rose appears complicated, but it is actually very easy to make with simple steps and a square paper. It is a nice and lovely ornament used to decorate a goddess costume or make a project at school.

It can also be decorated with paper leaves and ribbon, amongst other things.

Procedures

Step 1: Make a kite base.

Step 2: Loosen the upper triangle and pull it open.

Step 3: Flatten the loosed triangle, and lift the lower triangle.

Step 4: Open it and stretch it into a four, so it has a star-like look.

Step 5: Join the four tips to each other.

Step 6: Curl the tips round until it forms the shape of a rose.

Origami Card Holder

This cardholder is used to hold a business card or gift card on an office table or shelf. You can use a patterned gift wrap, graph paper, a paper bag, magazine pages, or origami paper. You can decorate the case with washi tape to present gift cards. There are different measurements used in making cardholders for business and gift cards. The measurement of a gift card holder is always larger, about 9 cm long.

Procedures

Step 1: Place the paper horizontally and fold it at the middle, then unfold it.

Step 2: Fold the two corners so that they close up the rectangle.

Step 3: Unfold it and fold the four edges slightly.

Step 4: Fold the corners back again.

Step 5: Turn the paper back and fold the top down.

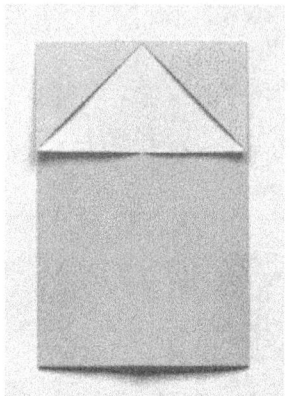

Step 6: Fold the down part upwards.

Your card folder is ready!

Bear Head

This project was made using a brown paper bag. It is a great project idea for little schoolboys. It is exciting and very thrilling. You need a large measurement of paper to make this model.

Procedures

Step 1: Fold your paper in half diagonally.

Step 2: Turn it again to the other direction and open it back up

Step 3: Take the top corner and fold it in about halfway

Step 4: Do the same to the other side.

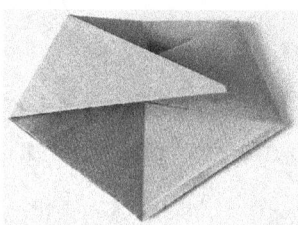

Step 5: Now fold the same corners back out the other direction. Fold the same corners down once and fold only one layer of the bottom corner up.

Step 5: Turn the whole thing over

Step 6: Fold the tip-up.

Step 7: Open up one side of the paper and fold it so that the top layer creases over the fold to create an area for the mouth.

You can go ahead to draw the ears, nose and mouth with a marker.

Wet Folding Project

This project is included to explain how the technique of wet-folding works. As explained in the previous chapters, the wet-folding technique is used to represent animate models on paper. This particular model is a dog folded with water. To wet fold a project, you don't need to wet the paper, but only moisturize it.

Procedures

Step 1: Fold the paper into the shape you intend to make.

Step 2: Spray the sheet with a little water from about 30cm away.

Step 3: Wipe the paper with a dry cloth to spread moisture evenly.

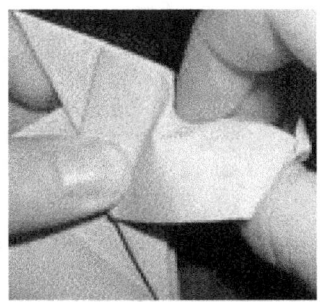

Step 4: Turn the other side of the sheet and moisturize it. The paper must not be wet; it should only be slightly damp to enable it to be malleable.

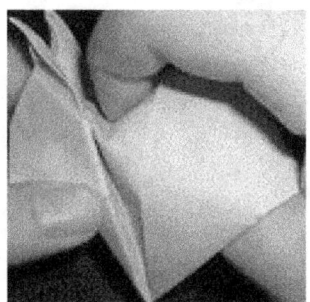

Step 5: Adjust all sides to give you the shape you desire. Fold or bend slightly, don't forcefully or roughly curve your paper; it could tear it apart.

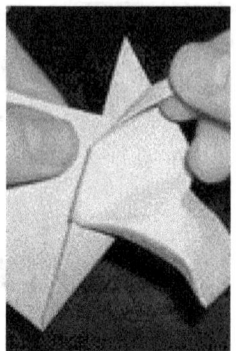

Step 6: Avoid using your fingertip to flatten the fold or cause an unnecessary impression.

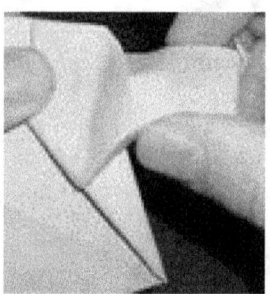

Step 7: After folding and adjusting the shape, use a rubber band to hold it in place.

Step 8: You can loosen the rubber once it is dry and your paper has fully taken shape. If your paper is yet to take shape, you can retry the wet-folding process again on the same paper or get a fresh paper.

The end... almost!

Hey! We've made it to the final chapter of this book, and I hope you've enjoyed it so far.

If you have not done so yet, I would be incredibly thankful if you could take just a minute to leave a quick review on Amazon

Reviews are not easy to come by, and as an independent author with a little marketing budget, I rely on you, my readers, to leave a short review on Amazon.

Even if it is just a sentence or two!

So if you really enjoyed this book, please...

\>\> Click here to leave a brief review on Amazon.

I truly appreciate your effort to leave your review, as it truly makes a huge difference.

Chapter 6

Frequently Asked Questions in Origami

Question: At what age can a child learn origami?

Answer: Origami can be learned at any age. You'll be surprised by the ability of young children to show creativity and innovative projects. Start preschoolers on origami patterns such as easy origami Tulips or Origami dogs.

These projects are very simple and encourage spatial recognition as well as symmetry. The projects involve very simple and short steps that they can easily remember. However, you shouldn't underestimate the ability of children's memories. Their memories could be as magnetic as sponges and very adaptive to the learn even more complex projects than you think. Paper boats, Fortune tellers and paper plane is a good place to start. It could be very beautiful for children to learn origami.

Nobody is too old to learn origami. As a young adult or an aging grandparent, you could always learn origami once you have the passion and desire. Everyone at any age of reasoning can learn origami and benefit from the mental exercise it gives you and the rest and relaxation it affords you. It could be a highly relaxing craft for an aging parent to help relax the muscles while having fun.

Question: Are all origami papers malleable?

Answer: No! all origami papers have different qualities. Some of them are more malleable than others because of the paper texture.

Question: How can I get original origami papers?

Answer: To avoid stories and prevent cheating when shopping for origami tools, try to buy papers made in Japan. They use non-toxic ink and this ink is directly applied to plain white paper. The ink then settles on the fibers of the paper, strengthening it well enough so that there is a smooth alignment of the paper when folded. The effect of this careful technology is that it leaves your paper smooth and prevents cracks during folds. It is no secret that Japan makes the best papers.

Question: What size of paper is best for me to use?

Answer: The more complex project you choose, the larger your paper should be. This is to provide an allowance for mistakes and extra creases, and creative tricks. Most of these tricks require a lot of paper. A traditional origami paper's regular size is 15cm, which is averagely fine for all projects. You should consider jumbo paper for very complex models.

Question: What is the best paper you'll recommend for beginners?

Answer: This question is commonly asked these days. As a beginner, many simple projects require just simple and straight forward steps that you can handle. These simple projects also require simple and easy to use tools. The best paper for origami that a beginner can use is the Standard paper. It is strong and very durable.

Question: Where can I store my origami tools?

Answer: Here is a very good question! Storage is very important in origami craft. Almost as important as the craft itself. It will be very heart-wrenching if, for any reason, you happen to lose your tools and materials due to carelessness. It could kill your motivation to practice. However, some persons are highly ignorant of this and tend to leave their things carelessly. The best way to store your tools is by creating a kit for them. You could either purchase one that is an already made plastic box or make one yourself with wood. What is important is that your tools are secured from water and oil. Most especially, you should be careful about where you keep your paper. Ensure that where it is stored, it won't get folded or be exposed to moisture. There is an already made paper storage box people used to store paper of all sizes. You could also consider a tall shelf for storage.

Question: Where is a perfect place to practice origami?

Answer: You do not need a workshop for origami, except you are going into it full time as a career, which you can only do when you become a master. As a beginner, all you need is a comfortable working space. You can build origami projects in your backyard or porch. Just like knitting, it is a simple and stress-free craft you can try out everywhere and anywhere. However, you have to be sure you are in a well relaxed and comfortable place, especially if you are working on a complex 3D project. You won't want to lose concentration and cause damage to your work. Here is my 2 cent advice, find a quiet place in your house and where you have a good amount of space to work. Most persons sit on the floor while they work; if that isn't comfortable for you, you can get a table and chair that is well balanced enough to allow you to work without stretching.

Ensure that the spot you are choosing is well lighted and ventilated. Ventilation will help you work comfortably, and light will allow you to work accurately and efficiently.

So, all I am saying is get a well comfortable and quiet place and furnish it with a small table and chair; you are good to go. If you have a library in your house, that is the perfect place you can consider.

Question: Is all paper folding origami?

Answer: Many scholars have argued this concept time after time, a large school of thought believes that origami is simply a paper-folding art using a square and with no other tools like adhesives and cuts. As I mentioned in the origami history, origami was the first paper folding art and started as a plain art with no cuts or adhesives, simply making folds with the hands. Today, origami and paper folding art has evolved. Whether it involves cutting or the use of adhesives, all paper folding arts are also addressed as origami.

Question: Is there a minimum and maximum age for children and adults to learn origami?

Answer: Origami is a craft for all ages. As long as the person has well-functioning motor and logical skills, they can be a paper folder. There is no age limit for little children to learn origami; if your child has a flair for creativity, origami is the easiest way to hone that skill. You can also introduce it to your child as little as five to start building creativity in them. Although some persons are naturally creative from birth, others had to learn creativity. It is best to teach them earlier through origami. However, when teaching a child, ensure that they don't put the paper in their mouth, which is very common with children. To prevent such occurrence, it is advised that you keep origami tools away from your child's reach till he/she clocks five. By then, the senses are well matured and coordinated. There are very simple models with easy steps that little children can make. The same goes for adults; aged people could practice this skill to engage and sharpen their locomotor and logical skills.

Question: What is the most commonly used origami base?

Answer: The bird base is the most common origami base. This base can be used to fold many models

Question: Can you fold a paper up to 7 times?

Answer: This is possible if you are using a big paper. Many paper folders love to fold their paper in half, many times to increase its density. However, if you make a fold many times, you make it difficult to make another fold. In other words, if your paper is very dense, you make it difficult for you to make other folds.

Conclusion

I congratulate you for completing this ride with me. You'll agree with me now that one unique thing about this art is its simplicity! Anyone can be a paper folder if you have the patience to learn the craft from scratch, make mistakes, learn from them and keep practicing. You should have learned that on the pages of this book.

However, it is one thing to be informed, and it is another thing to act on the knowledge you have received. Don't be in a hurry to move onto the next craft book without practicing what you have just read. I would have loved that you practiced while reading, but you need to practice hard and ensure that this knowledge is deeply rooted in you even now that you are done.

You could start from the simplest project or the making of basic folds with just flat paper and your two hands. Tools shopping can come later. Before you can become a master of anything, you need time and devoted practice, same with origami. To be a perfect origamist or paper folder, you need a concentrated time of endless practice and devotions.

Your first trials might not look good. Trust me; it is no big deal. You should applaud yourself for taking the courage to try something before beating yourself for not doing it well enough. What is important is that you enjoy the craft of paper folding and you are committed to learning. That is enough! Join patience to consistent practice and boom! You are an origami master.

Start from trying the folds on plain paper; you don't need to have a planned project before you start folding. We have listed a couple of basic origami folds for you; you could start trying them out and seeing what you can get out of them. You could also innovate your own designs of paper art. It only matters that you are trying out your creativity consciously and intentionally.

The journey is just starting, but believe me, if you keep by heart all the guidelines listed here, you'll be far ahead before you are even started.

Happy folding, origamists!

www.ingramcontent.com/pod-product-compliance
Lightning Source LLC
Chambersburg PA
CBHW050321120526
44592CB00014B/1995